ME COUNTING TIME

TIME From Seconds to Centuries

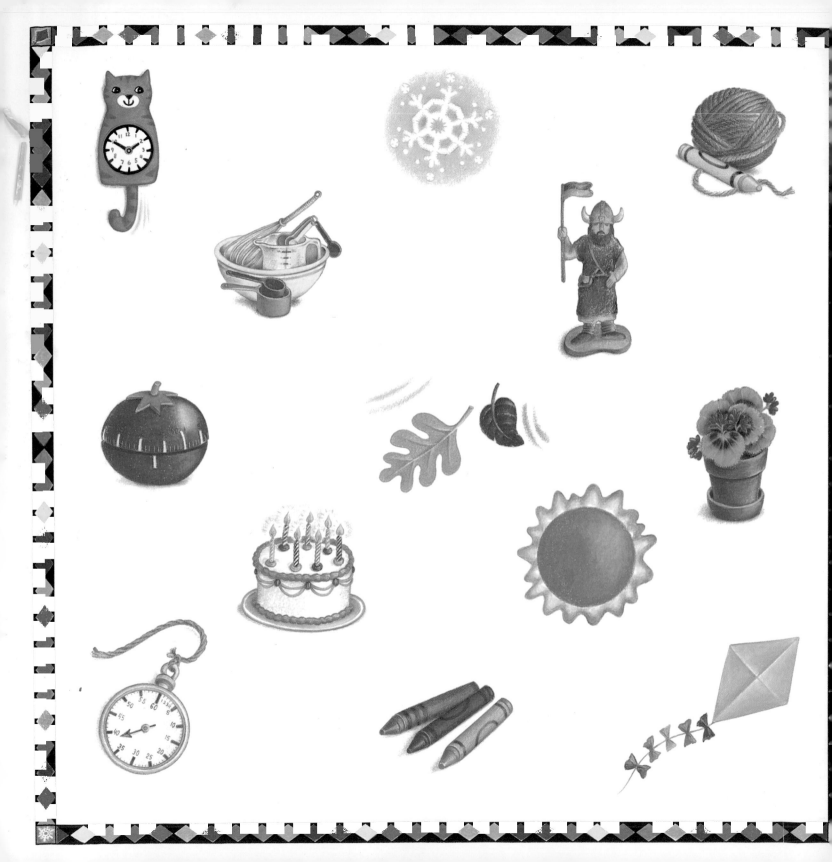

ME COUNTING
TIME

From Seconds to Centuries

by Joan Sweeney   illustrated by Annette Cable

Dragonfly Books —★ New York

For my brothers, Ed and Jim,
who gave me the answers I needed just in time!
—J.S.

For Grandma Myers,
love, A.C.

Text copyright © 2000 by Joan Sweeney
Illustrations copyright © 2000 by Annette Cable

Dragonfly Books with the colophon is a registered trademark of Random House, Inc.

Visit us on the Web! www.randomhouse.com/kids

Educators and librarians, for a variety of teaching tools, visit us at
www.randomhouse.com/teachers

Library of Congress Cataloging-in-Publication Data
Sweeney, Joan.
Me counting time / by Joan Sweeney ; illustrated by Annette Cable.
p.   cm.
Summary: Describes the relationship between a second, a minute, an hour, a day, a week, a month,
a year, a decade, a century, and a millennium as measurements of time.
ISBN 978-0-517-80055-3 (trade) — ISBN 978-0-517-80056-0 (lib. bdg.) — ISBN 978-0-440-41751-4 (pbk.)
1. Time—Juvenile literature. [1. Time. 2. Time measurements.] I. Cable, Annette, ill. II. Title.
QB209.5.S88   2000
529'.2—dc21   99022311

MANUFACTURED IN CHINA
15 14 13 12 11 10 9 8 7 6

This is me. I'm inviting my friends to my birthday party.
I'm going to be seven years old.

Just think—seven candles for seven years.
But a year isn't a candle, a year is a measurement of time.

Time comes in different amounts—seconds, minutes, hours, days, and more. Here's how I tell them apart.

First I think of the blink of an eye. That's about one second of time. I can count seconds by saying "one Mississippi, two Mississippi."

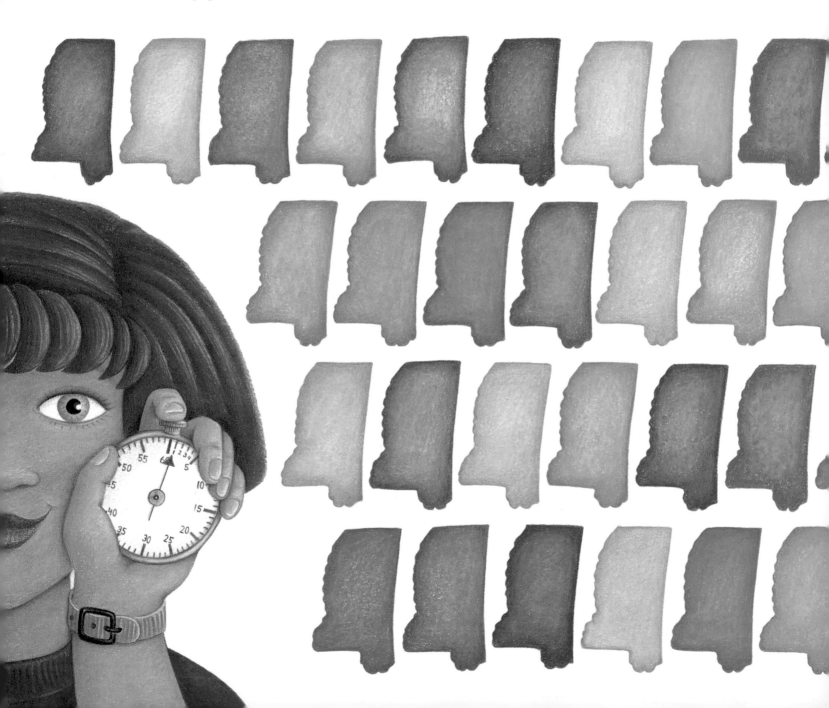

Then I think of *sixty seconds*. That's one minute of time.
I can write an invitation to my party in one minute!

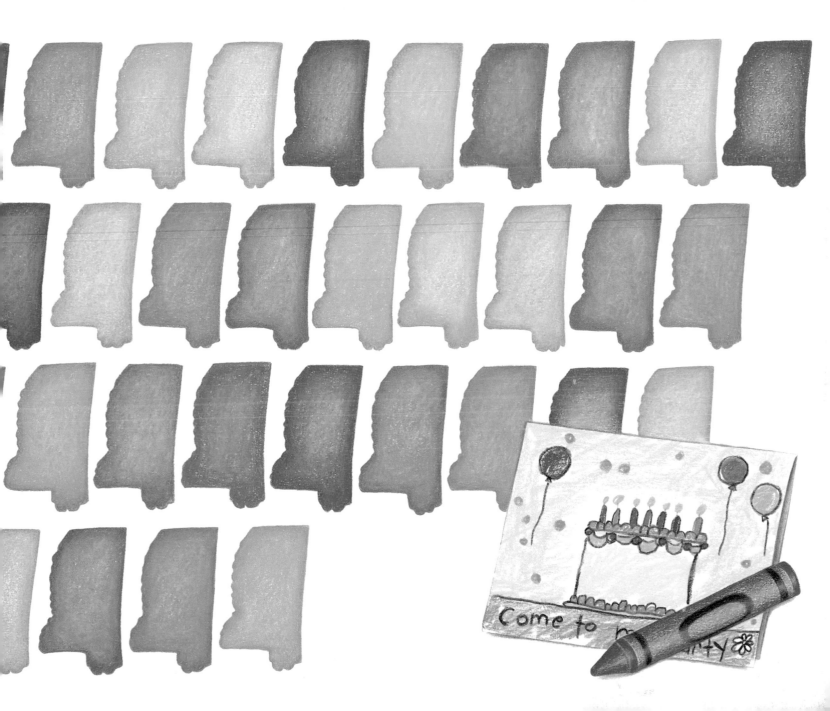

Then I think of *sixty minutes*. That's one hour of time—
the time it takes to make a birthday cake!

Then I think of *twenty-four hours*. That's one day.
The earth rotates once every day.

Then I think of *seven days*.
That's one week.

Sunday

Monday

Tuesday

Wednesday

Thursday

Friday

Saturday

Then I think of *four weeks*. That's about one month. Most months are just over four weeks. Only February is four weeks *exactly*—except during leap year. Then it's four weeks plus one day!

Then I think of *twelve months*. That's one year.
From winter to spring to summer to fall.

Then I think of *ten years*. Ten years is called a decade—
even longer than I've been alive.

And then I think of *ten decades*. One hundred years.
That's one century. Long enough for a tree to grow real tall.

A castle built in the year 1000.

Sand Castle, Virginia Beach 2000

Then I think of *ten centuries*. That's the same as one millennium. One thousand years!

Imagine. 31,556,926,000 blinks of an eye!
That's a long, long time.

A lot longer than seven years! So how do I get from
a millennium to my time? From a millennium to *now?*
Here's how.

A **millennium** ago, someone built a Viking ship like this. Now it would be one thousand years—ten centuries—old! A **century** ago, my great-great-grandpa had this picture taken. Now it's one hundred years old.

A **decade** ago, my nana sewed this wedding dress for my mother. Now it's ten years old.

A **year** ago, my family moved to our brand-new house.
Now it's twelve months old.

About a **month** ago, my cat had kittens.
Now they're four weeks old.

A **week** ago, I got new soccer shoes.
Now they're seven days old.

A **day** ago, I painted this picture.
Now it's twenty-four hours old.

My dad can make my birthday cake in one **hour**. An hour is sixty minutes. A **minute** is sixty seconds. And a **second** is like the blink of an eye.

In seven days, I'll be seven years old.
Seven candles. 220,898,482 blinks of an eye!

I can't wait for my party.
I'm going to have the time of my life!

TIME

60 seconds = 1 minute

60 minutes = 1 hour

24 hours = 1 day

7 days = 1 week

4 weeks = about 1 month

12 months = 1 year

10 years = 1 decade

100 years = 1 century

10 centuries = 1 millennium